My name is

▪ and ▪

MY
FAVORITE COLOR
IS
PURPLE

ILLUSTRATED BY MARIA NERADOVA

D1445393

odd
dot

New York

An imprint of Macmillan Children's Publishing Group, LLC
120 Broadway, New York, NY 10271 • OddDot.com

ILLUSTRATOR   **Maria Neradova**
DESIGNER   **Abby Dening**
EDITOR   **Daniel Nayeri**
ART DIRECTOR   **Timothy Hall**
CREATIVE DIRECTOR   **Christina Quintero**
PRODUCTION EDITOR   **Kathy Wielgosz**
MANAGING EDITOR   **Jennifer Healey**
PRODUCTION MANAGER   **Barbara Cho**

ISBN 978-1-250-76841-4

Our books may be purchased in bulk for promotional, educational, or business use. Please contact your local bookseller or the Macmillan Corporate and Premium Sales Department at (800) 221-7945 ext. 5442, or by email at MacmillanSpecialMarkets@macmillan.com.

DISCLAIMER: The publisher and authors disclaim responsibility for any loss, injury, or damages caused as a result of any of the instructions described in this book.

First edition, 2021
Printed in China by Hung Hing Off-set Printing Co. Ltd.,
Heshan City, Guangdong Province

1 3 5 7 9 10 8 6 4 2

Joyful Books for Curious Minds

NAME THAT PURPLE

There are so many shades of purple in the world that some of them don't even have names yet. What would you name these?

WHY PURPLE?

Purple is the greatest color in the world because . . .

But I also love it because . . .

Whenever I see purple, I feel . . .

When I'm sad, purple makes me . . .

When I'm happy, purple makes me . . .

_____ looks better when it's purple.

_____ tastes better when it's purple.

_____ should be purple.

PURPLE ROCKY MOUNTAINS
IN COLORADO, USA

LAVENDER FIELDS
IN FRANCE

WISTERIA TUNNEL
IN KITAKYUSHU, JAPAN

AMETHYST FROM
MINAS GERAIS, BRAZIL

JACARANDA TREES IN
CAPE TOWN, SOUTH AFRICA

SHIRAZ GRAPES FROM
SOUTH AUSTRALIA

COLOR YOUR BIG, PURPLE WORLD

WHAT'S THE DIFFERENCE?

There are twelve differences between these two pictures.
Can you spot them all?

FIND THAT PURPLE

Go on a purple scavenger hunt! Can you find these shades of purple in real life? Now draw pictures of the things you found!

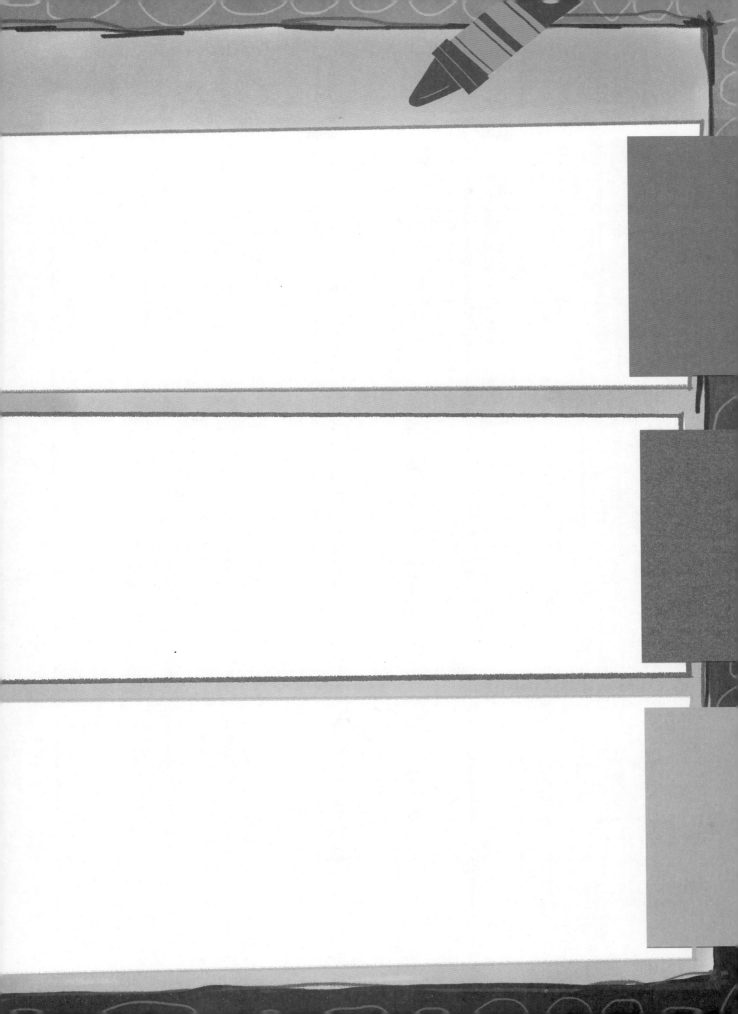

PURPLE-LICIOUS TREATS

PERFECT PURPLE SPRITZER

INGREDIENTS

3 cups purple grape juice

2 cups ginger ale

frozen purple grapes

DIRECTIONS

1. Mix grape juice and ginger ale together in a pitcher.

2. To serve, pour into glasses containing several frozen grapes.

3. Enjoy!

PURPLE COW MILKSHAKE

INGREDIENTS

2 cups frozen blueberries

1 cup milk

1 pint vanilla or strawberry ice cream

SPECIAL EQUIPMENT

blender

DIRECTIONS

1. Place all ingredients in blender and blend until smooth.

2. Pour milkshake into glasses.

3. Enjoy!

DYEING FOR PURPLE

Did you know that the stuff you have around the house can dye an egg your favorite color? It's true! With these ingredients, you can turn your eggs purple in no time!

YOU WILL NEED

- 4 cups purple grape juice
- 4 tablespoons white vinegar
- a pot with a lid
- a dozen hard-boiled white eggs
- a bowl or dish big enough to hold dye and eggs in a single layer
- tongs or slotted spoon
- egg carton

DIRECTIONS

1. Stir grape juice and vinegar together in pot.

2. Place eggs in bowl in a single layer and carefully pour dye over them. Make sure eggs are completely submerged.

3. Let eggs sit in dye overnight, covered, in the fridge.

4. Remove eggs from dye with tongs or slotted spoon and set them in carton to dry.

HIDDEN PURPLE

Lilac blossoms aren't the only thing you'll find in this shrub. Can you spot the ten things hiding here?

PURPLE DREAMS

If I could **HAVE** any purple thing, it would be . . .

If I could **EAT** any purple thing, it would be . . .

If I could turn **ANYTHING** purple, it would be . . .

f I could **SEE** any purple thing, it would be . . .

If I could turn **ANYONE** purple it would be . . .

If it were up to **ME**,

would all be purple.

MY PERFECT PURPLE OUTFIT

Draw your perfect purple outfit.

LUCKY PAPER STARS!

Use the paper strips on the right and follow the instructions to fold a skyful of lucky purple stars!

Start with a strip of paper approximately 11 inches long and ½ inch wide. Make a loose loop near one end of the strip.

Tie the loop into a knot and tighten gently so it makes a pentagonal (five-sided) shape.

 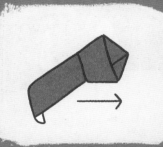

Tuck the short end into the pentagon. Then wrap the long end around the edge of the pentagon.

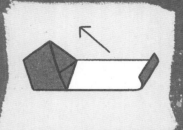

Continue turning and wrapping the long end around the pentagon. Don't press too hard.

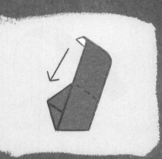

Repeat until you reach the end of the strip.

Trim any excess if necessary, then tuck the remaining length of strip into the pentagon.

Gently squish the sides of the pentagon to create creases between the five points using your finger nails. You now have a lucky paper star!

MUSEUM OF PURPLE

The paintings in the Purple Hall of Fame have been stolen! Can you re-create them?

The Slimiest Purple Snail

The Angriest Purple Monster

The Smartest Purple Dinosaur

A Magic Purple Potion

The Happiest Purple Pickup Truck

DRAW IT PURPLE

Follow the instructions to learn how to draw each purple creature.

BEETLE

1   2   3   4

SABI SABI
BIRD

1   2   3   4

MERMAID

1   2   3   4

BUTTERFLY

1   2   3

A-MAZE-ING PURPLE

There isn't just one way through this maze. Help each creature follow its path to the other side!

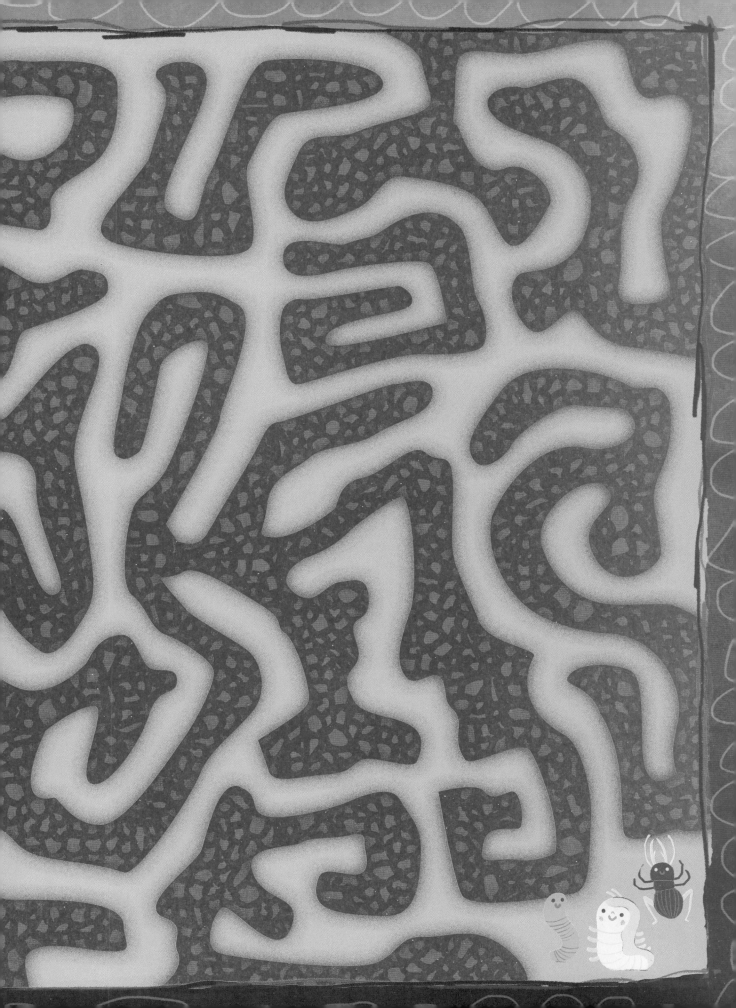

THE FACTS ABOUT PURPLE

PURPLE DOES NOT actually appear in a rainbow because it is a combination of red and blue, which are on opposite ends of the light spectrum.

CARROTS WEREN'T ALWAYS ORANGE.
A thousand years ago the majority of carrots were purple!

POTATOES, ASPARAGUS, BELL PEPPERS, and **CAULIFLOWER** all come in purple, too.

THE ANCIENT PHOENICIANS produced the first purple dye, extracted from sea snails, around the fifteenth century BCE. Mythology says the dye was discovered when a dog chomped on a sea snail and its mouth turned purple!

PURPLE GETS ITS NAME from the Latin *purpura*, which comes from *porphura*, the Greek word for those sea snails.

Because it took **TEN THOUSAND SEA SNAILS** to make one gram of dye, purple was very expensive, worth more than its weight in gold. Only the richest and most powerful could afford it, which is how it came to be thought of as the color of royalty.

MEDITATION ON PURPLE!

Color this design with every shade of purple you can find—then write your name in the center.

WHERE'S THAT PURPLE?

Can you find these particular shades of purple? Draw a line from each shade to where you see it in the picture.

TURN IT PURPLE

Pretty much everything should be purple, right? What in the world would you like to turn purple? Draw it here.

THE ART OF PURPLE

Complete the crosshatching to create your own three-dimensional amethysts!

 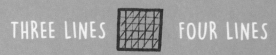

PAINT BY PURPLE

What color is this crown? Fill in the key at the bottom with your favorite shades of purple. Then color-by-number!

1 ○ 2 ○ 3 ○ 4 ○ 5 ○ 6 ○ 7 ○

A LOVE LETTER IN PURPLE

Let people know how much you love them—and purple! Cut out and fold this card and envelope, then write your message inside and send it to someone special.

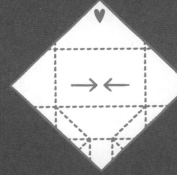

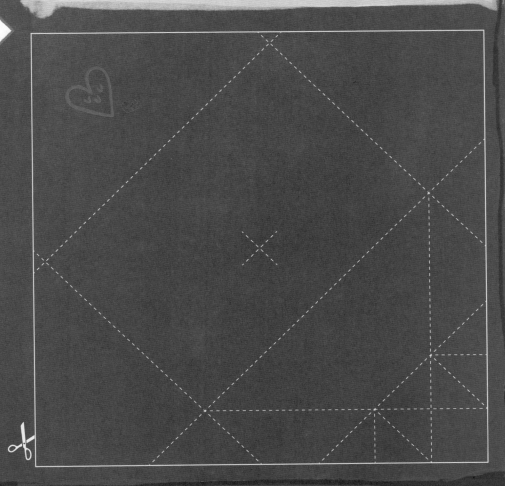

SEEING DOUBLE

These robots may all look the same, but only two are identical. Can you find them?

PURPLE CITY

Paint this town purple! Add your own buildings to the skyline.
Build on the samples you see here, or use your own imagination.

CONNECT THE PURPLE

Connect the dots with a purple marker or crayon to reveal this cool purple thing.

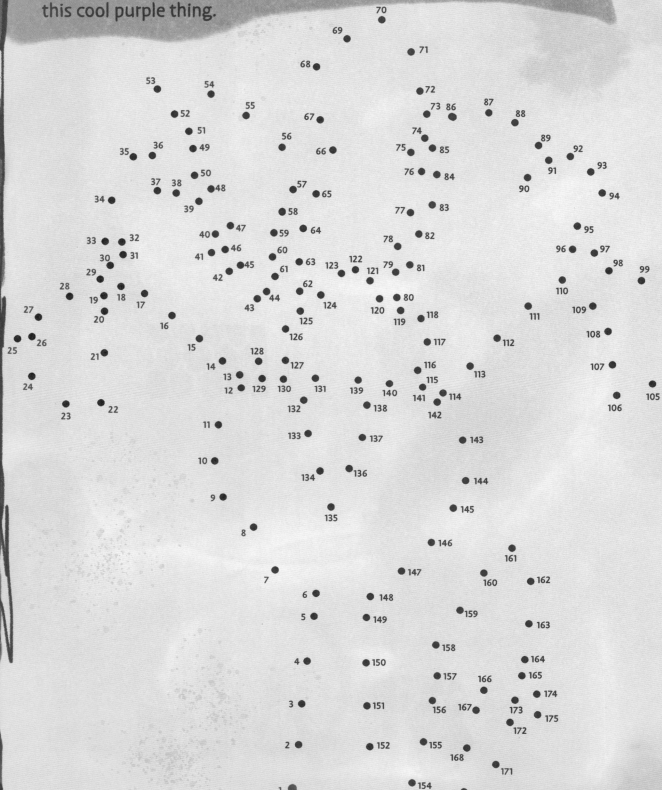

MY FAVORITE PURPLES

My favorite purple thing
IN THE WORLD is . . .

My favorite purple thing
I OWN is . . .

My favorite purple **FOOD** is . . .

My favorite purple **PLACE** is . . .

My favorite piece of purple **CLOTHING** is . . .

My favorite purple
ANIMAL is . . .

My favorite purple **DRINK** is . . .

My favorite **SHADE** of purple is . . .

My **SECOND-FAVORITE SHADE** of purple is . . .

PURPLE PAIRINGS

What are your favorite colors to pair with purple? Pick different colors to finish each picture and discover your favorite purple color combination!

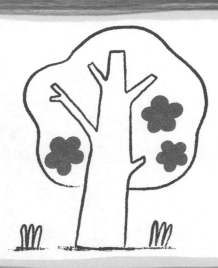

DO YOU WANT TO COME TO MY PARTY?

Throw a party with all purple things!
Cut out and fold these invitations, fill
in the details, and send!

YOU'RE INVITED
TO CELEBRATE
MY FAVORITE COLOR,
PURPLE!

Time:

Date:

Place:

Your friend,

YOU'RE INVITED
TO CELEBRATE
MY FAVORITE COLOR,
PURPLE!

Time:

Date:

Place:

Your friend,

YOU'RE INVITED
TO CELEBRATE
MY FAVORITE COLOR,
PURPLE!

Time:

Date:

Place:

Your friend,

PARTY GUEST

Learn how to assemble your party guest on the next page.

Who's going to be the
first guest at your party?
They'd better be wearing purple!
Follow the instructions to create
a party guest who can help you
welcome everyone else!

HOW TO ASSEMBLE YOUR PARTY GUEST

Cut out pieces along the solid lines.
Fold along the dotted lines.

Fold piece A by folding in the corners to bring edges together.

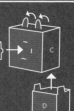

Assemble by matching up tabs and slots (tab A1 inserts into slot A1). Start by attaching piece A to C, then attach piece D to C.
Optional: Partially cut the ears and horns to fold them out.

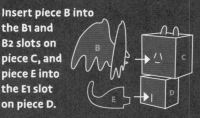

Insert piece B into the B1 and B2 slots on piece C, and piece E into the E1 slot on piece D.